W9-BNT-556

Latitude, Longitude, and Direction

JULIA J. QUINLAN

PowerKiDS press.

New York

Published in 2012 by The Rosen Publishing Group, Inc.
29 East 21st Street, New York, NY 10010

First Edition

Editor: Amelie von Zumbusch
Book Design: Greg Tucker

Photo Credits: Cover, pp. 4, 7, 8–9, 11 (bottom), 12–13, 16–17, 20 © GEOATLAS; pp. 5, 6 (left, right), 10, 11 (top), 13, 15, 17, 18, 19, 22 Shutterstock.com; p. 9 (right) BananaStock/Thinkstock; pp. 9 (left), 14 (left) iStockphoto/Thinkstock; p. 14 (right) Creatas Images/Thinkstock; p. 21 SSPL/Getty Images.

Library of Congress Cataloging-in-Publication Data

Quinlan, Julia J.
  Latitude, longitude, and direction / by Julia J. Quinlan. — 1st ed.
      p. cm. — (How to use maps)
  Includes index.
  ISBN 978-1-4488-6157-6 (library binding) — ISBN 978-1-4488-6272-6 (pbk.) —
  ISBN 978-1-4488-6273-3 (6-pack)
  1. Latitude—Juvenile literature. 2. Longitude—Juvenile literature. I. Title.
  QB224.5.Q85 2012
  526'.6—dc23
                                        2011021288

Manufactured in the United States of America

CPSIA Compliance Information: Batch #WW12PK: For Further Information contact Rosen Publishing, New York, New York at 1-800-237-9932

Contents

Different Directions

You can learn a lot about a place by looking at a map of it. Maps are also handy when you need to find your way from one place to another. However, a map will not be useful if you do not know which direction is which on it. North, south, east, and west are the major directions used

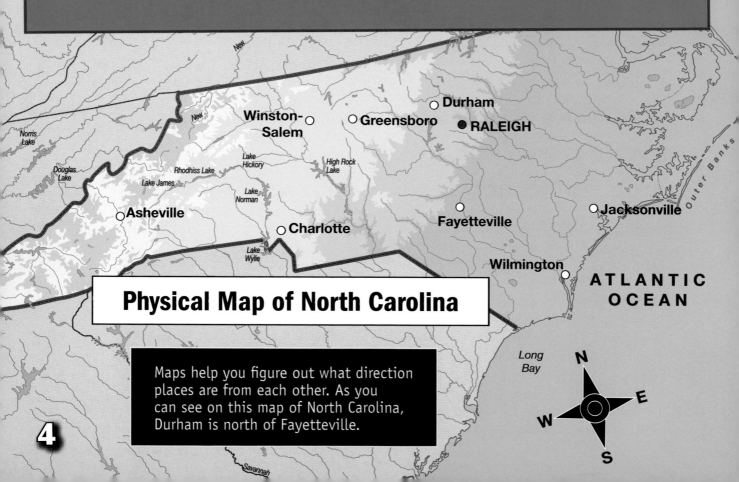

Physical Map of North Carolina

Maps help you figure out what direction places are from each other. As you can see on this map of North Carolina, Durham is north of Fayetteville.

These girls are studying a globe with their teacher. As many globes do, the globe they are looking at shows latitude and longitude.

on maps. There are also directions in between. These include northeast, southwest, southeast, and northwest.

Many mapmakers use latitude to measure how far north or south a place is. They use longitude to measure how far east or west somewhere is.

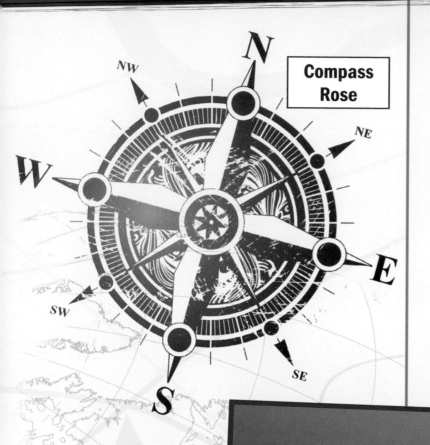

Compass Rose

A compass rose is a **symbol** that shows which way north, south, east, and west are on a map. It has points that show each direction.

To use a map, you may also need to figure out which direction is which in real life. One way to do this is to look at the Sun. It rises in the east and sets in the west.

No matter where you are, the Sun always sets in the west.

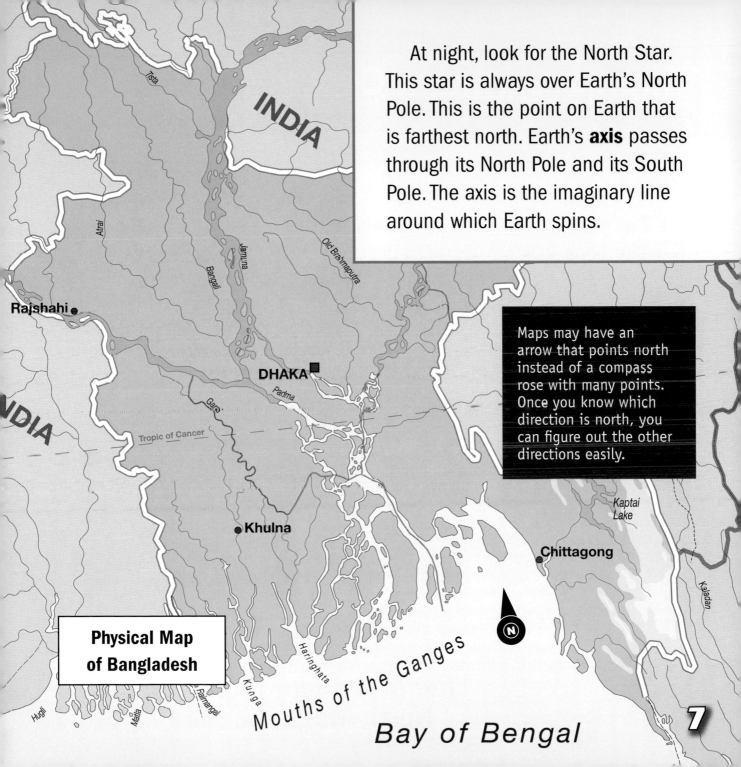

At night, look for the North Star. This star is always over Earth's North Pole. This is the point on Earth that is farthest north. Earth's **axis** passes through its North Pole and its South Pole. The axis is the imaginary line around which Earth spins.

Maps may have an arrow that points north instead of a compass rose with many points. Once you know which direction is north, you can figure out the other directions easily.

Physical Map of Bangladesh

INDIA

INDIA

Tista

Atrai

Jamuna

Bangali

Old Brahmaputra

Rajshahi

DHAKA

Padma

Garo

Tropic of Cancer

Khulna

Kaptai Lake

Chittagong

Kaladan

Haringhata

Kunga

Mouths of the Ganges

Hugli

Malta

Raimangal

Bay of Bengal

BERING SEA

A **compass** is a tool that shows which way north is. A compass has all of the directions on it. A **magnetized** needle sits over the directions. To figure out which direction is north, line up the needle's point with north on the compass. The needle always points to Earth's **north magnetic pole**.

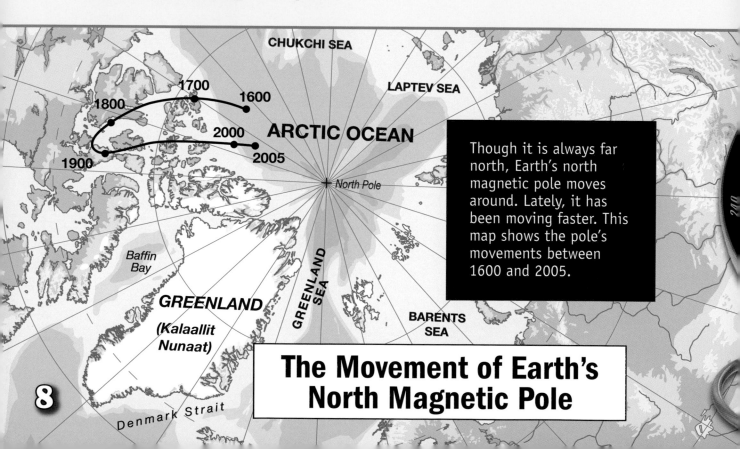

CHUKCHI SEA

LAPTEV SEA

1700
1800
1600
2000
ARCTIC OCEAN
1900
2005

North Pole

Baffin Bay

GREENLAND
(Kalaallit Nunaat)

GREENLAND SEA

BARENTS SEA

Denmark Strait

Though it is always far north, Earth's north magnetic pole moves around. Lately, it has been moving faster. This map shows the pole's movements between 1600 and 2005.

The Movement of Earth's North Magnetic Pole

8

Earth's north magnetic pole and the North Pole are near each other. This means that you can use a compass needle that points to the north magnetic pole to determine north from most places. The compass will not show true north if you are very far north, though.

Compasses do not always look the same. The point of the needle in the compass to the left is green. The compass the kids to the right are using has an arrow-shaped needle.

What Is Latitude?

Lines of latitude are imaginary lines that go around the world. They run from east to west. There are 180 lines of latitude. The lines are also called **parallels**. Parallels are measured in degrees. The symbol ° stands for "degrees." The **equator**, which runs around the center of Earth, is the 0° parallel. There are 90 parallels north of the equator and 90 parallels south.

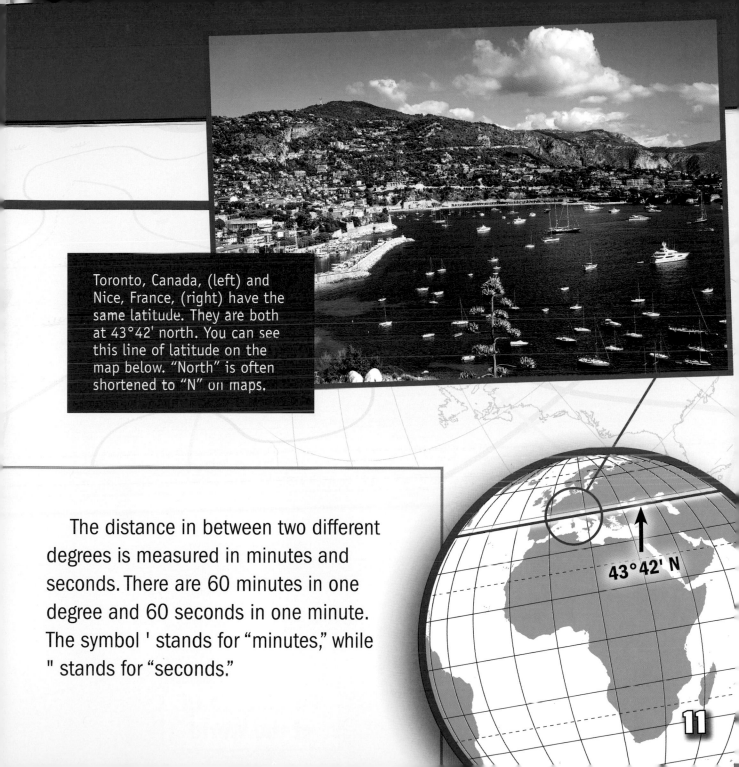

Toronto, Canada, (left) and Nice, France, (right) have the same latitude. They are both at 43°42' north. You can see this line of latitude on the map below. "North" is often shortened to "N" on maps.

The distance in between two different degrees is measured in minutes and seconds. There are 60 minutes in one degree and 60 seconds in one minute. The symbol ' stands for "minutes," while " stands for "seconds."

43°42' N

Important Parallels

The equator separates Earth into two **hemispheres**, or halves. The Northern Hemisphere is north of the equator, while the Southern Hemisphere is south of it.

There are other important parallels, too. The Tropic of Cancer is located at 23.5° north, while the Tropic of Capricorn is at 23.5° south. Between

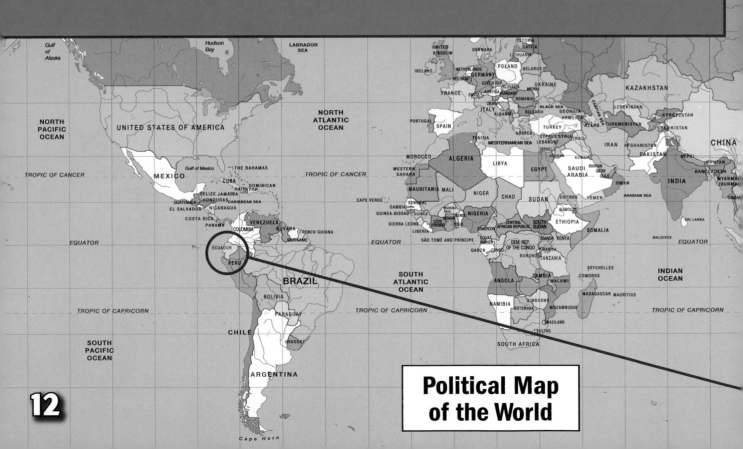

Political Map of the World

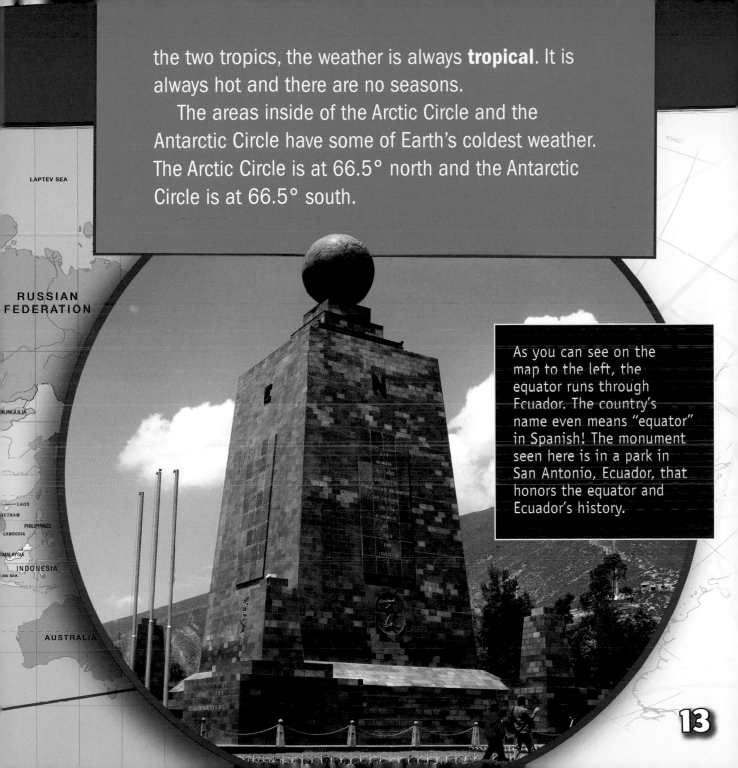

the two tropics, the weather is always **tropical**. It is always hot and there are no seasons.

The areas inside of the Arctic Circle and the Antarctic Circle have some of Earth's coldest weather. The Arctic Circle is at 66.5° north and the Antarctic Circle is at 66.5° south.

LAPTEV SEA

RUSSIAN FEDERATION

MONGOLIA

LAOS

VIETNAM

PHILIPPINES

CAMBODIA

MALAYSIA

INDONESIA

JAVA SEA

AUSTRALIA

As you can see on the map to the left, the equator runs through Ecuador. The country's name even means "equator" in Spanish! The monument seen here is in a park in San Antonio, Ecuador, that honors the equator and Ecuador's history.

The History of Latitude

Latitude was invented by the Greeks over 2,000 years ago! They divided the world into parallels. They came up with the equator, the Tropic of Capricorn, and the Tropic of Cancer.

People have known how to measure latitude for thousands

Top: Maps have used latitude for a very long time. *Right*: This sailor is using a sextant. People measure the angles of objects in the sky with sextants. They can then figure out their latitude.

This is an astrolabe. In the past, sailors used astrolabes to measure the angles of objects in the sky. Once they knew this, they could figure out their latitude.

of years. They measured the positions of objects in the sky, such as the Sun. Then they used math to figure out their latitude. Starting in the 1500s, sailors from Europe began exploring the world more. They needed to know their exact latitude to figure out where they were and where they were going. People invented tools that made it easier to measure latitude.

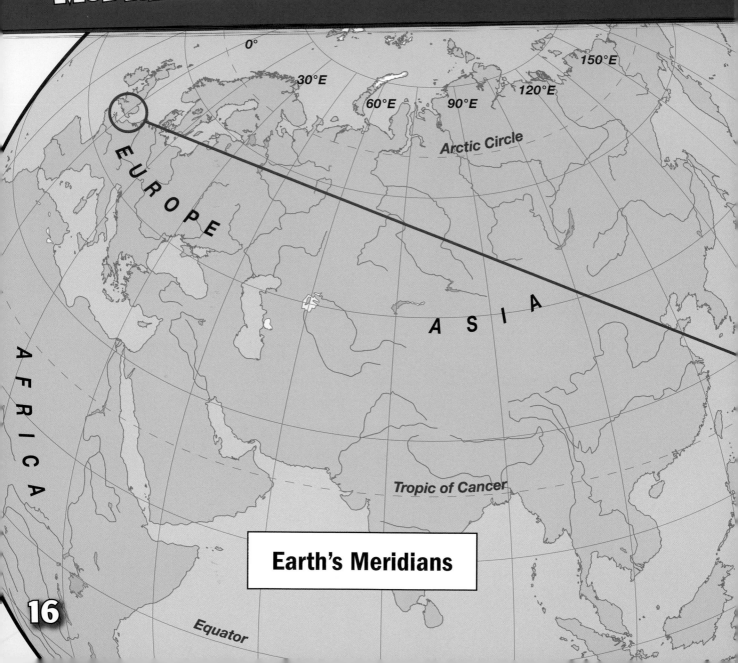

0°

30°E

150°E

60°E

120°E

90°E

Arctic Circle

EUROPE

ASIA

AFRICA

Tropic of Cancer

Earth's Meridians

16

Equator

Lines of longitude are called **meridians**. Meridians run up and down Earth, from north to south. They meet at the North Pole and at the South Pole. There are 360 meridian lines. Meridians are measured in degrees. Like parallels, they can be broken down into minutes and seconds.

The prime meridian is at 0°. It is located over Greenwich, England. The 180th meridian is on the opposite side of Earth from the prime meridian. These two meridians divide the world into the Eastern Hemisphere and the Western Hemisphere. The Eastern Hemisphere is east of the prime meridian. The Western Hemisphere is west of it.

PACIFIC
OCEAN

The prime meridian runs through the Royal Observatory, in Greenwich, England. *Map:* The distance between meridians is greater near the equator than it is near the Arctic Circle.

Breaking Up Time

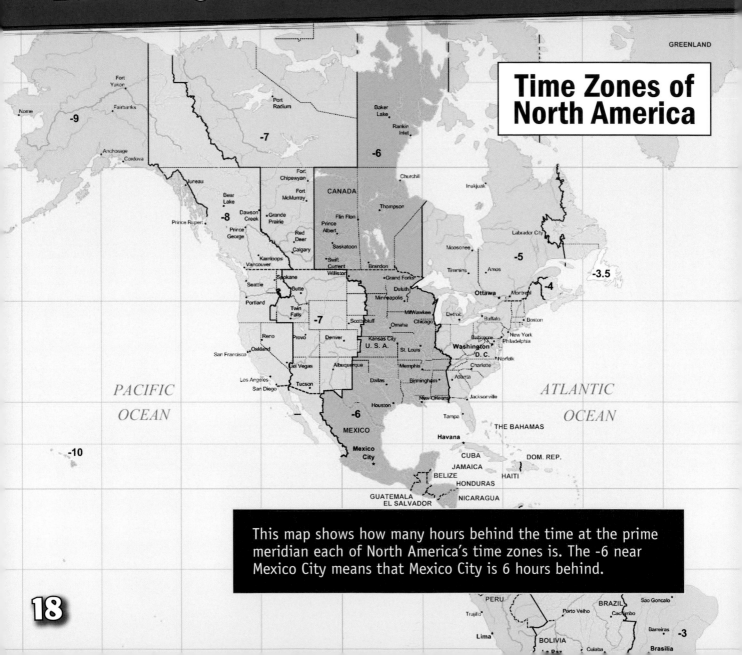

Time Zones of North America

This map shows how many hours behind the time at the prime meridian each of North America's time zones is. The -6 near Mexico City means that Mexico City is 6 hours behind.

The international date line is important. Places west of it are one day ahead of places to its east. For most of its length, the line runs along the 180th meridian. It zigzags so that countries can stay on the same side of the line, though.

Meridians were also guides for Earth's **time zones**. Time zones are places where clocks are set to the same time. California and New York are in different time zones. When it is 3:00 p.m. in New York, it is 12:00 p.m. in California. Over water, each time zone is 15° wide. Over land, time zones sometimes run along nearby political borders instead.

Sometimes countries decide to switch from one side of the international date line to the other. Samoa, seen here, has done this.

Longitude was very hard to figure out. It was so hard that, in 1714, the British government offered a reward to anyone who could find a better way to figure longitude. In 1759, clockmaker John Harrison solved the problem by making a better watch.

The borders of several US states are based on the American meridian, which ran through Washington, D.C. The border between Colorado and Utah is 32° west of this meridian.

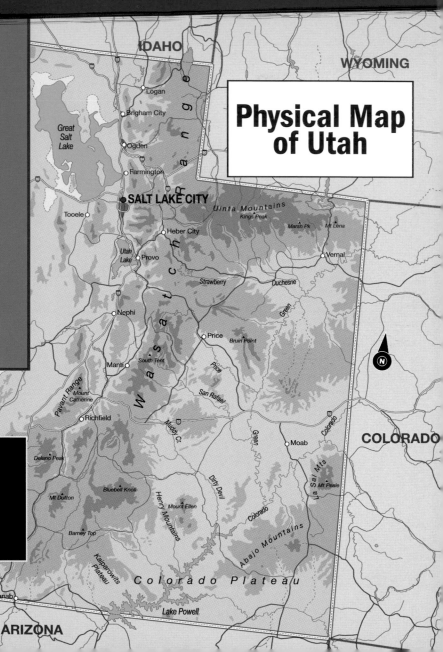

Physical Map of Utah

IDAHO

WYOMING

Logan

Brigham City

Great Salt Lake

Ogden

Farmington

SALT LAKE CITY

Tooele

Heber City

Uinta Mountains
Kings Peak

Marsh Pk

Mt Lena

Utah Lake

Provo

Vernal

Strawberry

Duchesne

Green

Nephi

Price

Bruin Point

Manti

South Tent

Price

San Rafael

Payant Range
Mount Catherine

Muddy Cr.

Green

Colorado

Richfield

Moab

COLORADO

Delano Peak

Dirty Devil

La Sal Mts
Mt Peale

Mt Dutton

Bluebell Knoll

Henry Mountains
Mount Ellen

Colorado

Barney Top

Abajo Mountains

Kaiparowits Plateau

Colorado Plateau

St. George

Kanab

Lake Powell

Fort Pierce Wash.

NEVADA

Frisco Pk

ARIZONA

This painting of John Harrison shows him holding the watch he invented. The watch was called a marine chronometer. People most often used it to figure out longitude while at sea.

People set the watch to the time at a known longitude. They figured out the time it was where they were by looking at the Sun. They used the difference in times to **calculate** their longitude.

Longitude did not have a natural starting point. For a long time, different countries used different prime meridians. As countries worked together more, this became confusing. In 1884, 25 countries came together and chose Greenwich, England, for the prime meridian.

Unseen but Important

The lines of latitude and longitude are not real lines on Earth. They were made up by people. People worked long and hard to come up with a way to describe how far north, east, south, or west any place on Earth is. Latitude and longitude were important to people exploring the world for the first time. They are still important now.

Understanding latitude and longitude helps us understand where we are in the world. It makes traveling easier and can help you if you get lost.

You can use latitude and longitude to describe the exact location of any place on Earth. For example, the Pyramids of Giza, in Egypt, are 29°58'45" north and 31°08'04" east.

Glossary

axis (AK-sus) A straight line on which an object turns or seems to turn.

calculate (KAL-kyuh-layt) To figure out something by doing math.

compass (KUM-pus) A tool made up of a freely turning magnetic needle that tells which direction is north.

equator (ih-KWAY-tur) The imaginary line around Earth that separates it into two parts, northern and southern.

hemispheres (HEH-muh-sfeerz) Halves of a round object.

magnetized (MAG-neh-tyzd) Made something magnetic. Magnetic things are drawn toward or away from each other.

meridians (meh-RIH-dee-unz) Imaginary lines that run north and south and break Earth into 360 equal parts.

north magnetic pole (NORTH mag-NEH-tik POHL) The point to which all compasses point.

parallels (PAR-uh-lelz) Imaginary lines that run east and west and break Earth into 180 equal parts.

symbol (SIM-bul) An object or a picture that stands for something else.

time zones (TYM ZOHNZ) Areas that have their clocks set to the same time.

tropical (TRAH-puh-kul) Having to do with the warm parts of Earth that are near the equator.

Index

Web Sites

Due to the changing nature of Internet links, PowerKids Press has developed an online list of Web sites related to the subject of this book. This site is updated regularly. Please use this link to access the list:
www.powerkidslinks.com/maps/latit/